Caz Can See Nan

By Carmel Reilly

Mum and Caz go
to see Nan.

Caz can get on a big jet!

Caz zips up her bag.

Mum zips up her bag, too.

Mum and Caz get a bus at six.

The sun was not up yet.

Mum and Caz run in.

Fix the bag tags here, Mum!

Caz

Mum and Caz jog
to get the jet.

Do not go yet, jet!

The jet revs and revs.

It zips up, up, up!

On the jet, Caz gets a bun.

It is yum!

Mum gets a big cup.

Yes! Here is Nan!

Nan and Caz hug.

CHECKING FOR MEANING

1. How did Caz and Mum travel to see Nan? *(Literal)*

2. Where did Mum fix the tags? *(Literal)*

3. Why does the jet rev before it takes off? *(Inferential)*

EXTENDING VOCABULARY

zips	What are the two meanings of *zips* in this book?
yet	What does *yet* mean in this book? What are the sounds in this word? If you take off the *y*, what other letter can you put at the start to make a new word?
Fix	Sometimes the word *fix* means to mend something that is broken. What is the meaning of the word *fix* in this text?

MOVING BEYOND THE TEXT

1. Have you ever travelled on a plane or a jet?
    Where did you go? Who went with you?

2. Why do you need to put a tag on your bag?

3. Where are bags stored on a plane?

4. Do you think Nan was pleased to see Caz?
    How do you know?

SPEED SOUNDS

Xx	Yy	Zz				
Kk	Ll	Vv	Qq	Ww		
Dd	Jj	Oo	Gg	Uu		
Cc	Bb	Rr	Ee	Ff	Hh	Nn
Mm	Ss	Aa	Pp	Ii	Tt	

PRACTICE WORDS

zips

Caz

yet

six

yum

Fix

Yes